With Needle and Thread

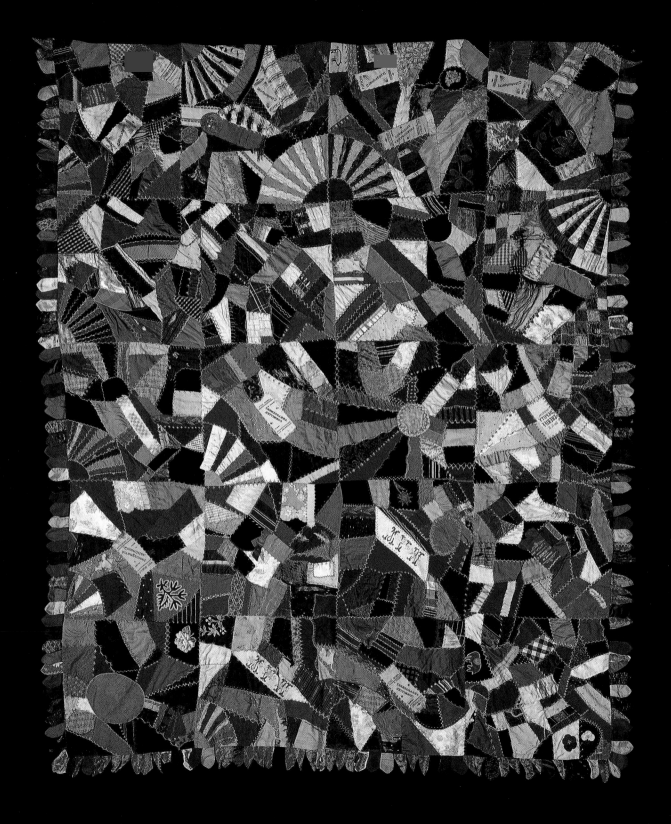

With Needle and Thread

A BOOK ABOUT QUILTS

Raymond Bial

Houghton Mifflin Company
Boston New York 1996

Acknowledgments

Many people helped in the preparation of this book, notably Betty Casad, Charles Casad, Sally Duchow, Dan Eaton, Ruth Eaton, Barb Frazier, Cheryl Kennedy, Debbie Langendorf, Nancy McDonald, Barbara McGee, Naomi Rempe, and Sue Richter. I would also like to express my appreciation for the cooperation of the following groups and organizations: Douglass Center, Early American Museum, East Bend Mennonite Church, Illini Country Stitchers, Illinois State Museum, Rockome Gardens, Sears, Roebuck and Company Archives, Vermilion County Museum, and the ladies of the Methodist church in Havana, Illinois. I am especially grateful to Cheryl Kennedy and the Early American Museum for the use of their quilt photographs, all of which were taken by Wilmer Zehr.

Copyright © 1996 by Raymond Bial

All rights reserved. For information about permission to reproduce selections from this book, write to Permissions, Houghton Mifflin Company, 215 Park Avenue South, New York, New York 10003.

For information about this and other Houghton Mifflin trade and reference books and multimedia products, visit The Bookstore at Houghton Mifflin on the World Wide Web at (http://www.hmco.com/trade/).

Manufactured in Singapore
The text of this book is set in 14/21 Adobe Caslon
Book design by S. M. Sherman

Frontispiece: Crazy quilt made by Sarah Lindsay of Galesburg, Illinois, in 1898. (Courtesy Early American Museum)

TWP 10 9 8 7 6 5 4 3 2 1

Library of Congress Cataloging-in-Publication Data
Bial, Raymond.
    With needle and thread : a book about quilts / Raymond Bial.
       p. cm.
       Includes bibliographical references.
       Summary: Examines quilts and quiltmaking as an artistic expression, handed down through generations of women.
    ISBN 0-395-73568-8
    1. Patchwork — United States — History — Juvenile literature. 2. Quilting — United States— History — Juvenile literature. 3. Patchwork quilts — United States — History — Juvenile literature. [1. Patchwork. 2. Quilting. 3. Quilts.] I. Title.
TT835.B48   1995   746.46'0973 — dc20
95-16416   CIP   AC

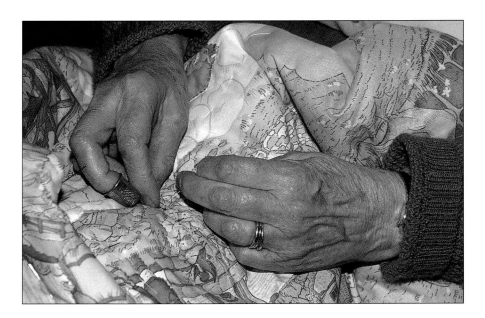

This book is respectfully dedicated to the generations of women

who have brightened the world with their lovely quilts.

This book is intended to be a sampler of the role that quilts play in the lives of individuals, families, and cultures. Virtually every person with whom I spoke as I was working on *With Needle and Thread* told me a story about quilts made by a grandmother, mother, sister, or friend. I also have vivid memories of the Flower Garden quilt that adorned my own grandparents' bed. I don't know the history of that quilt or what happened to it after the death of my grandfather, but one of my earliest and favorite photographs was of that quilt. Every time I look at that photograph I remember my grandparents and many wonderful visits to their home.

People from many cultures have been making quilts for hundreds of years — from Asia, Europe, and more recently North America — and quilts are woven into the fabric of our lives. Around the world quilting is enjoying a resurgence, especially in the United States. There has been a long history of quiltmaking in Appalachia, and equally strong traditions are being rediscovered from New England to the West Coast. But quilting is more than its past; quiltmaking is a dynamic art, with groups, from the Amish to African Americans to the Hmong people of Southeast Asia, continually bringing their distinctive traditions to the craft. Several hundred patterns exist, and new styles are continually created.

Over the years quilts have come to be valued in many ways: they keep children warm on winter nights; they are carefully stored in cedar

chests and closets to be passed down as family heirlooms; and they are hung as works of art in museums. Quilts may help us to better understand the history of women as well, including their contributions to many social causes.

Like a quilter myself, I carefully selected and arranged key "pieces" of text and photographs to make this book into a lovely and orderly patchwork. Certainly the number and variety of quilt patterns are remarkable, often breathtaking, but I wanted *With Needle and Thread* to be more about people and their connection to quilts. Feelings about quilts run deeply through the quilters' lives, and it is this abiding love and respect for quilts and quiltmaking that I have sought to evoke in *With Needle and Thread: A Book about Quilts.*

"What with rearin' a family, and tendin' a home, and all my chores —
that quilt was a long time in the frame. The story of my life is pieced into
it. All my joys and all my sorrows." — West Virginia quilter, circa 1970

For centuries women throughout the world have spent their "spare time" making quilts. In the hands of women, this basic skill became a homegrown art form, with quilters taking pride in their own abilities and respecting the work of others. Moreover, women didn't have many rights or opportunities, and quilting allowed them to express themselves through their work. "Women didn't have much of a say, except through their sewing," explains a contemporary quilter, Debbie Langendorf. Despite society's restraints and many other hardships, women were able to craft beautiful quilts.

Many of the quilt patterns that have been invented over the generations have colorful names: Album Patch, Bowtie, Brick Wall, Broken Dishes, Chinese Coins, Crosses and Losses, Diamond in the Square, Double Shoofly, Flower Garden, Monkey Wrench, Nine Patch, Ocean Wave,

Flower Garden is a popular pattern. The patches in this quilt by Nettie Bell Redkey of Byron, Illinois, circa 1930, form colorful flowers. (Courtesy Early American Museum)

Paving Block, Railroad Crossing, Star of Bethlehem, Sunshine and Shadow, Trip around the World, Tumbling Blocks, Windmill Blades, and Young Man's Fancy. In addition, there is the crazy quilt, which can be made in just about any design. There are literally hundreds of quilt patterns, nearly all of which were created and named by quilters themselves. Other unique styles include all-white quilts, single-piece quilts, and solid-color quilts. There are also pictorial quilts that show actual scenes. Most quilts are considered folk art because they are made by ordinary people in cities and towns across the country — and around the world.

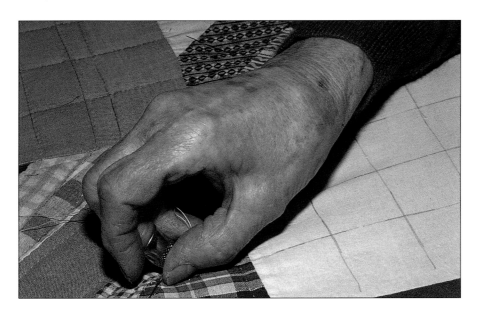

Above: Thousands of tiny hand stitches are needed to sew a quilt. This quilter wears a thimble to protect her finger from the sharp needle.

Opposite: Quilters often vary patterns. This Eccentric Nine Patch, by an anonymous quilter in the late 1800s, is based on the Nine Patch pattern. (Courtesy Early American Museum)

Above: With each generation, family quilts become more deeply valued. This antique quilt has been safely tucked away in a cedar chest.

Opposite: Women regularly gather in the basement of the East Bend Mennonite Church to make quilts for the Mennonite Relief Sale. Concern for those in need has long been a central theme of quiltmakers.

A quilt may grace a bed in an upstairs room or, having been passed down from a grandmother, may be carefully folded and stored away. Family quilts are often made for special occasions, such as a daughter's wedding or the birth of a baby. And as the years go by, these quilts become cherished family heirlooms. Quilts may also be made "for the public," meaning they will be sold. Often quilts are raffled off or sold at auctions to raise money for charities.

These women regularly volunteer many hours of their time to make quilts.
This quilt will be raffled off to support a charitable cause.

Traditionally, quilting circles or bees offered women a
chance to share the labor; these women also met for friendship and good conversation. Quilts require a great deal of
work, and a sense of cooperation and community often made
it more enjoyable to undertake the detailed work. Women
still get together in church basements and elsewhere to prac-
tice their art — but they may also work alone at home, or
sometimes late in the evening after their children have gone
to sleep. Today many men also enjoy quilting, and quilters
are found in large cities as well as small towns.

Quilts consist of three layers: a top, batting in the middle, and a backing (also called a lining). Quilt tops and backings may be made of wool, linen, silk, cotton, or, more recently, synthetic fabrics. The batting or filling is usually wool or cotton. Over time two primary methods of quilting have evolved: pieced and appliquéd. Pieced, or patchwork, quilts consist of bits of cloth sewn together, most often in blocks or squares. Appliquéd quilts have cloth sewn directly to a top that is a single layer of fabric. Patchwork became

This quilt edge shows the top, batting, and backing. Modern batting comes in sheets, so not as much quilting is needed. In the past, every inch or two of the quilt had to be sewn to hold the loose cotton batting in place.

the more popular method of quilting in pioneer days when fabric was precious and, out of necessity, women had to use every scrap. Patchwork remains the primary method of quilting today.

Quilts are made by cutting a pattern out of paper, which is then transferred to the cloth by "marking" — tracing the pattern outlines — with chalk or a pencil. The cloth is then cut out and the pieces sewn, or "pieced," together. Batting is

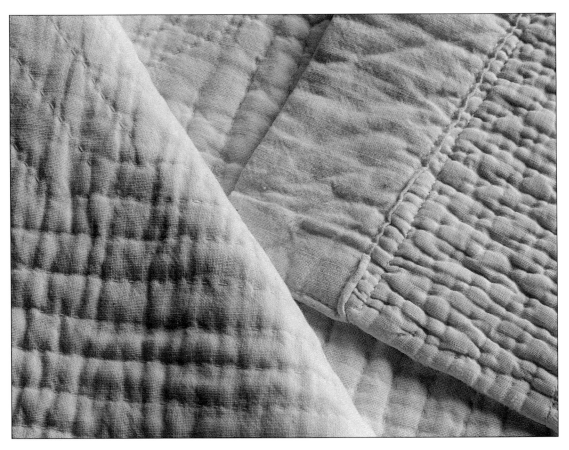

This detail of a quilt backing and edges shows the delicacy of the stitches. Called "betweens," quilting needles are usually small to enable fine work.

Quilts require small stitches to make perfectly straight lines and intricate patterns, such as the swirling shapes of these flower petals.

placed between the backing and the top to form a kind of sandwich, and the pieced top, batting, and backing are stitched together. This stage is called quilting. Quilting stitches must be small enough to follow the straight or curved lines of the design and to hold the quilt together through many years of use. Once the quilting is finished, the edges are sewn closed. Quilters often stretch unfinished quilts on frames, especially when they are working as a group. Sometimes part of a quilt will be placed in a hoop to be worked on one block at a time. This technique is called lap quilting.

Quilting in one form or another has been popular for thousands of years. The first known depiction of quilting is from 3400 B.C., a carved figure of an Egyptian pharaoh wearing a quilted garment. It is believed that decorative quilting came to Europe from Asia during the Crusades (A.D. 1100 – 1300), a likely idea because textile arts were more developed in China and India than in the West. The earliest known bed quilt dates from fourteenth-century Sicily. Quiltmaking was also very popular in India in the sixteenth century, and there is a long tradition of quiltmaking in Great Britain as well as other European countries.

The first Europeans to cross the Atlantic Ocean brought quilts and the craft of quilting with them. Quilts were popular in Colonial America, and they made their way westward through the Appalachians and out onto the prairie. Folded and tucked into chests, quilts bumped along in Conestoga wagons following the Oregon and Santa Fe trails to the Pacific Ocean.

Until the Industrial Revolution in the mid-1800s, women raised sheep for wool and grew their own flax and cotton. They spun thread, wove fabric, and sewed clothing, household linen, and quilts. Girls learned to quilt from an early age; with fabric so valuable it was an essential skill.

This young girl works diligently on her first quilt block. Note the batting between the backing and the top. Mothers once routinely taught their daughters the art of quilting.

"Before I was three years old, I was started at piecing a quilt. Patchwork, you know. My stint was at first only two blocks a day, but these were sewn together with the greatest care or they were unraveled and done over," Marion Nicholl Rawson (1878 – 1956) recalled.

From 1840 to the time of the Civil War, America was rapidly changing due to westward expansion and industrial technology; people were either moving to cities or heading to the frontier. During this period, album quilts became especially popular. Also called "autograph" or "friendship" quilts, they reflected the separation of friends and family. These quilts were first made in small areas of Pennsylvania and Maryland, but soon album quilts became widely popular. Each one was cherished because it included the quilter's own words, signature, or some other remembrance, similar to an autograph album. Every woman left a clear memory of herself in the stitches and in her request to "forget me not."

As people left the east for an uncertain future on the frontier, quilts provided a link with loved ones left behind, whom they might never see again. Quilts were put to good use for warmth and for wrapping treasured items in wagons and to cushion the hard wooden seats. Quilts were also required in all difficult situations — births, deaths, illnesses,

Some quilts were named for the journey west: Rocky Road to Kansas, Oregon Trail, and this quilt made by Emma Fleming, circa 1930, called Road to California. (Courtesy Early American Museum)

Each of the circles in this autograph quilt was signed by one of its quilters, who stitched their signatures into the quilt with needle and thread.

and injuries. Those who died along the way were wrapped in quilts and buried at trailside. Quilts also served as remembrances of loved ones lost.

Once they'd settled in new homes, pioneer women got together in quilting bees. Although, in the words of one Texas settler, they might attempt "to out-rival each other in the daintiness of the stitches . . . they helped each other in every way." Women also sought to bring a sense of culture, if not refinement, to those isolated lands.

Quilts were put to good use in log cabins and sod houses against the hardships of everyday life on the frontier. Winters were often long and bleak, and the colorful quilts helped to provide a little warmth and brightness in the crude and drafty shelters. It is not surprising that the Log Cabin pattern was popular at this time.

Odessa Wilman recalled the quilts her pioneer mother made at the turn of the century in their underground home: "Mama's best quilts were her dugout quilts because that was when she really needed something pretty. She made a Butterfly and a Dresden Plate and a Flower Basket during those two years in the dugout. After a while she got used to

As people moved west, they brought their quilts with them. From log cabins to frame houses, this Ocean Wave quilt has been in the family for several generations.

the sound of the wind, if it didn't go on too long, and she could get real soothed with that sound and the needlework at night sitting by the lamp."

"Back in the old days we had to make the quilts so thick. You know in those old dugouts the wind come through so bad that you really had to be covered to sleep," said Lois Hand, recalling her childhood in the late 1800s on the plains of Texas.

Early quilts were all handmade, but in 1846 Elias Howe, Jr., patented the sewing machine. An invention of great significance, it became widely used in the next two decades. "By this invention the needlewoman is enabled to perform her labor in comfort; tasks that used to require the midnight watches — and drag through perhaps 20 hours, she can now complete in two or three," stated the editor of *Godey's Lady's Book* in 1860. However, to this day, it is the care and skill of sewing by hand that are most admired in a quilt.

Over the course of the nineteenth century many women became active in a series of causes, starting with charities and missionary work associated with churches. Often denied other means, women increasingly used quilting to make political statements and to raise funds for causes.

Log Cabin was a favorite design of settlers. Although this quilt made by Illini Country Stitchers in 1988 is varied by flowers and vines, it has the classic rows of stitched logs. (Courtesy Early American Museum)

Quilts helped keep slaves warm in their cabins. Slaves often made quilts in traditional patterns for their masters; when the quilts became worn, they were given back to the slaves.

Some became deeply involved in efforts to abolish slavery. The renaming of Job's Tears to Slave Chain expressed the opposition of many northern women to the "peculiar institution." From the 1830s to the start of the Civil War, women sponsored fairs and bazaars in which they sold their needlework, including quilts, to raise funds for the abolition movement. The first Anti-Slavery Fair was held in Boston in 1834 and was so successful that it became an annual event. During the Civil War, women contributed thousands of quilts to keep soldiers warm or to be raffled to provide money for the war effort. The tradition continued during both the Spanish-American War and World War I as quilters again worked to supply the country's fighting forces. Wartime quilting continued up to the advent of World War II. For this conflict, many women on the home front put aside their needle and thread to become an important part of the labor force.

Women involved in the abolition movement began to refer to the quilt pattern Jacob's Ladder as The Underground Railroad. Its contrasting light and dark squares came to symbolize the dangers of the escape routes.

In the latter half of the nineteenth century, women became active in the Women's Christian Temperance Union, crusading against the consumption of alcohol. A quilt pattern called Drunkard's Path appeared in large numbers during these years. Similarly, quilts were made in support of the cause of woman suffrage.

In the late 1800s, the crazy quilt also became extremely popular. This style expressed the restless spirit of rebellion among women, because no set pattern had to be followed. Crazy quilts likely did reflect the emerging independence that paralleled support for progressive causes such as women's education and child welfare throughout this dynamic period. Yet these quilts were also very practical, especially among poor women who couldn't afford to waste a single scrap of fabric.

During the Great Depression, quilters more than ever emphasized bright colors and pretty designs in the face of hard times. Since the early twentieth century, quilt patterns published in books and magazines, such as *Farm and Fireside,* and weekly editions of local newspapers had been widely distributed. This resulted in a greater availability of patterns. Rather than a few patterns handed down or learned from friends, a quilter had many choices, creating renewed interest in quilting and new variations.

This Wheel Spoke quilt was made by the Women's Christian Temperance Union of Harvard, Illinois, in 1889 to raise funds to end alcohol consumption in the United States. (Courtesy Early American Museum)

Above: The winning World's Fair quilt is shown held by a contest official (center) and two other women. (Courtesy Sears Archives)

Opposite: This modern crazy quilt by Irene Boyer of Springfield, Illinois, illustrates the spirit and imagination of the best of this style. (Courtesy Early American Museum)

The popularity of quiltmaking reached a peak when Sears, Roebuck and Company sponsored the Century of Progress quilt contest in conjunction with the 1933 Chicago World's Fair. A staggering 25,000 quilts were entered into competition. Ironically, only recently was it discovered that Margaret Caden didn't make the winning quilt she entered. She hired three women to sew the quilt for her, but never credited their work or shared the prize money with them. The quilt was given to Eleanor Roosevelt and has since been lost.

Historically, women planted gardens, canned fruits and vegetables, raised chickens, and made quilts for their families. However, during the Depression women had to be especially thrifty and self-reliant. It became more necessary than ever to fashion quilts from pieces of worn-out dresses and shirts, but even scraps came to be in short supply. Along with old clothing, quilters began to use feed sacks. Farmers usually returned feed sacks, but mill owners, not wishing to clean and store the sacks, began to sell them back to customers for a few cents. Millers' associations even printed booklets with ideas for using the sacks. In the early 1940s, Georgia Swanner made striking quilts from feed-sack cloth: "I had eight quilts and tops made to go when I married. In the country you could sleep under four or five quilts in one of those houses." Even tobacco pouches and cigar premiums were made into quilts, while homegrown cotton served as filling. Quilting became a way to survive hard times.

The tradition of quiltmaking has been especially important in the mountains of Appalachia. Quiltmaking strengthened families and communities. "There are times a quilt's a way of sayin' welcome — a quilt for a new neighbor, or a new bride, or a new baby. We been doin' that sort of thing all our lives," a contemporary Appalachian quilter explained.

Virtually any cloth can find its way into a quilt. Around 1900, Hannah Crose of Iuka, Illinois, used old flour sacks to piece a quilt. (Courtesy Early American Museum)

Above: With a few simple tools — needle, scissors, and thimble — quilters are able to transform plain cloth into lovely objects of enduring value.

Opposite: Quilters have always been inventive at finding fabric. An anonymous quilter (most likely from Missouri) used tobacco premiums to make this remarkable quilt. (Courtesy Early American Museum)

Another quilter from West Virginia observed, "This quilt's a piece of livin' history. It speaks to me in voices long passed away."

Quiltmaking also gave poor rural women a means of expressing themselves. "The gift for quilting is like the gift for music. You have to love it. It's *borned* in you," one mountain quilter pointed out.

Like other rural women, the Amish have also depended upon quiltmaking as a rare opportunity for self-expression. They have, in fact, become so well known for their quilts that it is often assumed they have a long history of quiltmaking. Actually, their first quilts date only from the 1830s, and the most striking Amish quilts were made from the 1880s to the 1960s. Curiously, their quilts are created within a community that discourages art. The Amish do appreciate beauty, however, as long as it has a practical use. Thus, handcrafted quilts are not only permitted, but widely admired. Quiltmaking also fits the Amish work ethic and emphasis upon group activities.

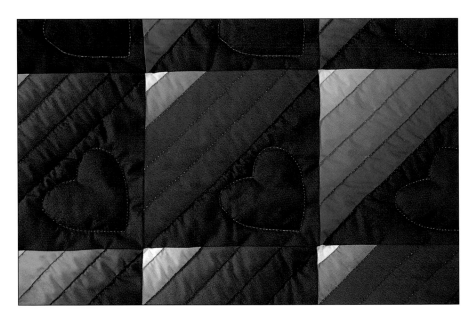

This Amish Shadow pattern reflects the Amish emphasis on black and bright colors. Because this quilt was made for sale, hearts may appear in the design; quilts for Amish homes may not use representational designs.

Amish women make all of the family's clothes, and the bright fabric scraps reappear in their quilts.

Highly prized, Amish quilts are used to adorn beds or are offered for sale to supplement the income of their large families. Living in a traditional culture, the Amish make quilts as gifts on formal occasions, notably weddings and births, and as expressions of friendship. An Amish woman may make a "namesake quilt" as a gift for a girl in the community with whom she shares a common first name. The Amish also make quilts for fundraisers, such as the Mennonite Relief Sale, to benefit others in their own community or distant charities.

Above: This quilt of Bible stories was made by Harriet Powers in the late 1800s. (Bequest of Maxim Karolik, courtesy Museum of Fine Arts, Boston)

Opposite: African-American quilters often improvise their patterns, as in this striking satin quilt by Pauline Pelmore of Champaign, Illinois.

African Americans also have a distinguished tradition of quiltmaking. Early quilts made by slaves should not be confused with true styles of African-American quiltmaking. Familiar patterns are followed by African-American quilters, but two primary themes persist: the use of strong, colorful patterns and storytelling. Story quilts, such as those by Harriet Powers, are compelling; however, bold designs in vivid colors, similar to African textiles, are the foremost examples of African-American quiltmaking today.

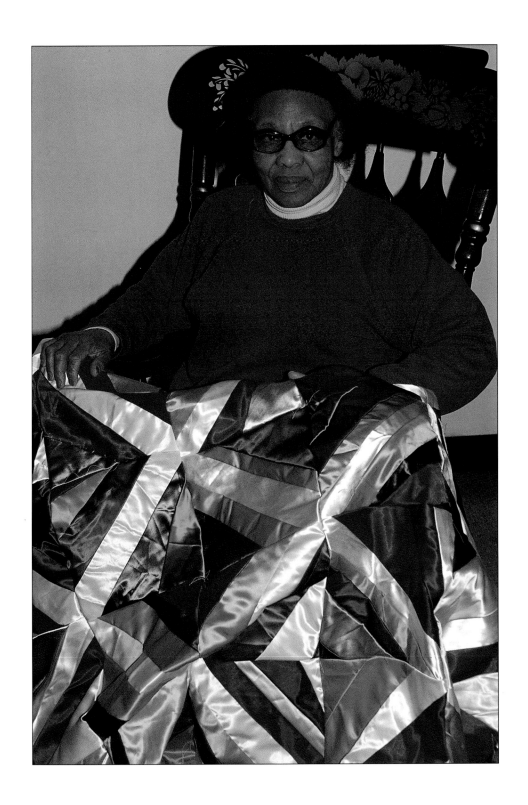

At the end of the Great Depression, many American women gave up quiltmaking when they left the home to work in factories during World War II. Gradually, many people came to prefer the latest styles in clothing, automobiles, and housewares. There was such an emphasis on modern products that many cherished family quilts were forgotten in the attic or even given away. The turning point came in 1971 with a quilt exhibition at New York's Whitney Museum of American Art. With this event, quilts began to be viewed not only as a craft, but also as an art form.

A few years later, during the 1976 Bicentennial celebration, interest in history and family genealogy led to a further revival of interest in quilts. In an age full of technological

Today quilts are often hung as works of art in museums. These quilts are sometimes called "wall quilts" to distinguish them from those intended for everyday use.

Constance Berg of Good Hope, Illinois, made this pictorial quilt to commemorate the country's two hundredth birthday. (Courtesy Early American Museum)

wonders, many people have also been drawn back to handicrafts, including quilts and quiltmaking. And no longer must precious fabric be hoarded for quilts. With the renewed interest in quilting, a variety of fabrics and battings as well as all-cotton thread for hand sewing are widely available. There are even quilting specialty stores. Quilts have again become valued as personal objects, most often as family heirlooms passed down in an unbroken tradition from one generation to another. "I had my quilt up at the library and someone offered me a thousand dollars," said Naomi Chartier, a quilter from Havana, Illinois. "But I wouldn't sell it. I want my daughter to have this quilt when I'm gone."

Many different quiltmaking traditions continue to run through American culture — not only Appalachian, Amish, and African-American styles but also a multitude of patterns and variations that are handed down from quilter to quilter in cities and small towns throughout the country. And with the revival of the art of quilting come new traditions and new voices. Quiltmaking is continually enriched by the new designs and contributions of immigrant groups. Recent immigrants such as the Hmong people of Southeast Asia have brought their own distinctive style of quiltmaking to the United States.

This quilt by an anonymous Hmong quilter illustrates a new style in American quiltmaking, reflecting the distinctive tradition of these mountain people of Southeast Asia. (Courtesy Early American Museum)

The tradition of quiltmaking as social or political expression is also finding a place in modern times. The AIDS Memorial Quilt has helped stir public awareness and concern both for those who are ill and for those who have died of the disease. The powerful album quilt is a sixteen-ton patchwork of three-by-six-foot blocks covering fourteen acres. Quilted by friends and family, each block includes personal mementos in honor of those who have fallen victim to AIDS.

Composed of more than 30,000 panels, the AIDS Memorial Quilt illustrates the enormity of the epidemic. (Courtesy NAMES Project Foundation: Marcel Miranda III, photographer)

"Quilts give women an opportunity to speak across the generations," explains Cheryl Kennedy of the Illinois Documentary Quilt Project. About this unfinished family quilt she says, "I never knew my grandmother very well, but I can get to know her through the quilt."

Quilters continue to believe in the value of their work. As Mary White, a contemporary Texas quilter, stated, "You're just given so much to work with in a life and you have to do the best you can with what you got. That's what piecing is. The materials is passed on to you or is all you can afford to buy . . . that's just what's given you. Your fate. But the way you put them together is your business. You can put them in any order you like. Piecing is orderly. First you cut the pieces, then you arrange your pieces just like you want them."

Reflecting the creative spirit and the diversity of peoples, quilters are active the world over. Quilting again flourishes and will most certainly be passed on to yet another generation. As Polly Dixon reflected on a lifetime of quilting that began during the Great Depression: "I love to piece quilts. It's a joy. It's an art within."

QUILT DETECTIVES

Information about many quilts has been lost over time. It may not be known when or where a particular quilt was made or even by whom. However, the evidence of each anonymous quilter's life is stitched into her quilt — in the needlework, the fabric from which the quilt was made, and the pattern.

In 1981, the Kentucky Quilt Project collected information about hundreds of quilts in that state. An exhibit followed, and subsequently almost every state initiated a similar project to identify and describe as many quilts as possible before their history was completely lost. So far, tens of thousands of quilts have been identified and registered across the country. Much of the work in these projects has been undertaken by unpaid volunteers who wish to have this art form preserved and the quiltmakers recognized for their remarkable work.

FURTHER READING

The following books were consulted in the preparation of *With Needle and Thread:*

Barker, Vicki, and Bird, Tessa. *The Fine Art of Quilting.* New York: E. P. Dutton, 1988.

Burdick, Nancilu B. *Legacy: The Story of Talula Gilbert Bottoms and Her Quilts.* Nashville, Tenn.: Rutledge Hill Press, 1988.

Cooper, Patricia, and Buferd, Norma Bradley. *The Quilters: Women and Domestic Art.* Garden City, N.Y.: Anchor Press, 1978.

Elbert, E. Duane, and Kamm, Rachel. *History from the Heart: Quilt Paths across Illinois.* Nashville, Tenn.: Rutledge Hill Press, 1993.

Ferrero, Pat, and Hedges, Elaine. *Hearts and Hands: The Influence of Women and Quilts on American Society.* San Francisco: Quilt Digest Press, 1987.

Fons, Marianne, and Porter, Liz. *Quilts from America's Heartland: Step-by-Step Directions for 35 Traditional Quilts.* Emmaus, Pa.: Rodale Press, 1994.

Granick, Eve Wheatcroft. *The Amish Quilt.* Intercourse, Pa.: Good Books, 1989.

Houck, Carter. *The Quilt Encyclopedia Illustrated.* New York: Harry N. Abrams, 1991.

Kolter, Jane Bentley. *Forget Me Not: A Gallery of Friendship and Album Quilts.* Pittstown, N.J.: Main Street Press, 1985.

Lewis, Alfred Allan. *The Mountain Artisans Quilting Book.* New York: Macmillan, 1973.

Mosey, Caron L. *America's Pictorial Quilts.* Paducah, Ky.: American Quilter's Society, 1985.

Orlofsky, Patsy, and Orlofsky, Myron. *Quilts in America.* New York: McGraw-Hill, 1974.

Pellman, Rachel, and Pellman, Kenneth. *Amish Crib Quilts.* Intercourse, Pa.: Good Books, 1985.

———. *A Treasury of Amish Quilts.* Intercourse, Pa.: Good Books, 1990.

Waldvogel, Merikay. *Soft Covers for Hard Times: Quiltmaking and the Great Depression.* Nashville, Tenn.: Rutledge Hill Press, 1990.

Webster, Marie D. *Quilts: Their Story and How to Make Them.* 1915. Reprint, Detroit: Gale Research Co., 1972.

Zegart, Terri. *Quilts: An American Heritage.* New York: Smithmark Publishers, 1994.

Several quotes in *With Needle and Thread* were drawn from the following books: *The Mountain Artisans Quilting Book, The Quilters: Women and Domestic Art, Soft Covers for Hard Times: Quiltmaking and the Great Depression*, and *Quilts in America.*